THE
DOG OWNER'S
SURVIVAL GUIDE

SOPHIE JOHNSON
ILLUSTRATED BY **TATIANA DAVIDOVA**

summersdale

THE DOG OWNER'S SURVIVAL GUIDE

Illustrations by Tatiana Davidova

An Hachette UK Company
www.hachette.co.uk

Summersdale Publishers Ltd
Part of Octopus Publishing Group Limited
Carmelite House
50 Victoria Embankment
LONDON
EC4Y 0DZ
UK

www.summersdale.com

Printed and bound in China

ISBN: 978-1-80007-400-2

Substantial discounts on bulk quantities of Summersdale books are available to corporations, professional associations and other organizations. For details contact general enquiries: telephone: +44 (0) 1243 771107 or email: enquiries@summersdale.com.

TO ....

FROM.............................

INTRODUCTION

Puppers. Fur babies. Doggos.
Our love for dogs is unconditional,
which is lucky really, as they
don't always make life smooth
sailing. They're what gets us
out of bed in the morning (must
they bark so early?) and what
we think about last thing at
night (again with the barking?).

So, here is your survival guide to life with a dog. Tips, tricks and advice to make life as a dog parent as enjoyable as can be. Because though they put us through hell sometimes, life with a dog is just heavenly.

ALWAYS KEEP TOILET
SEATS FIRMLY CLOSED
IF YOU DON'T WANT
IT TO BECOME YOUR
DOG'S FAVOURITE

COCKTAIL LOUNGE.

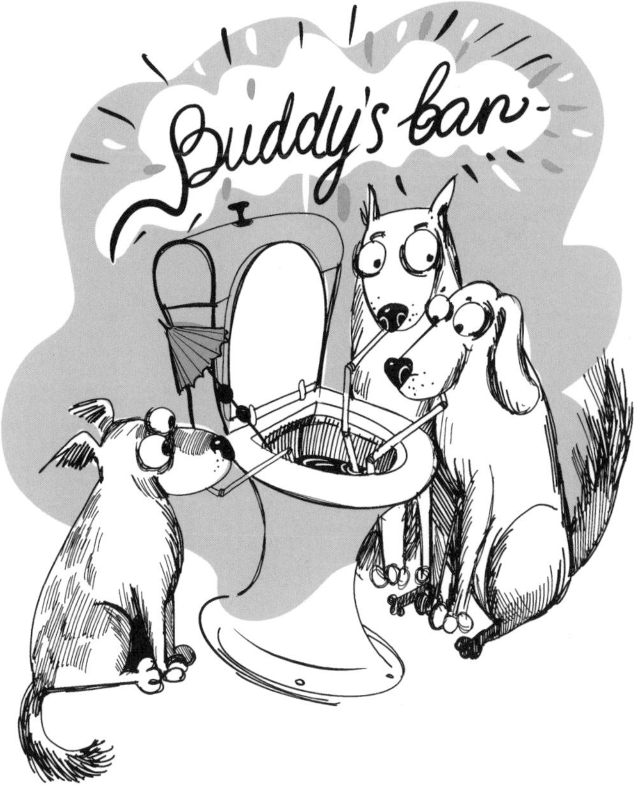
Buddy's bar

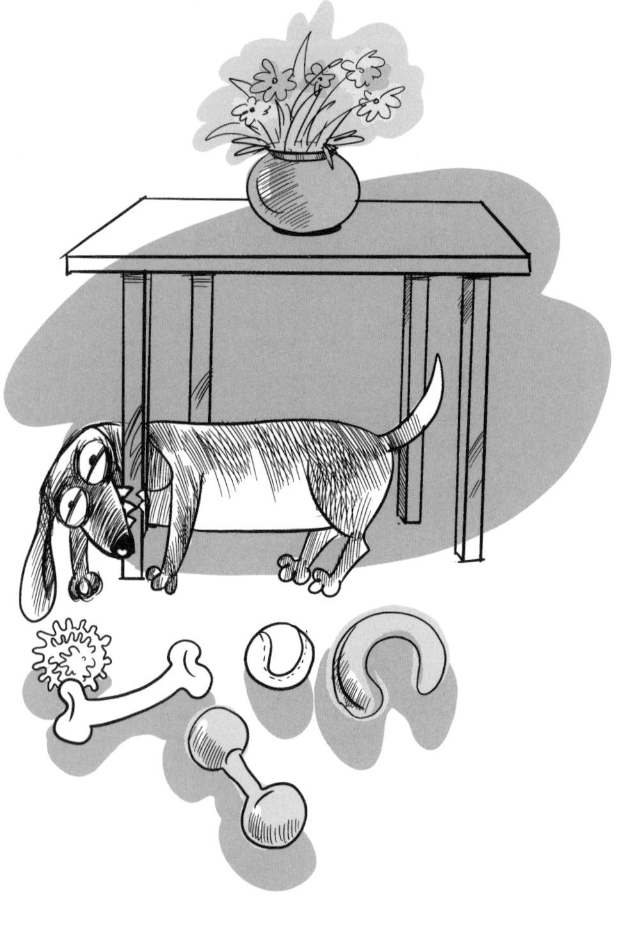

NO MATTER HOW MUCH MONEY YOU SPEND ON FANCY TOYS FOR YOUR DOG, THEY WILL ALWAYS FIND SOMETHING MUCH MORE FUN TO CHEW ON – JUST BE GLAD IT'S NOT YOUR FINGER.

START WORKING
ON YOUR MENTAL
TOUGHNESS – THOSE
PUPPY-DOG EYES
ARE ENOUGH TO
BREAK EVEN THE
ICIEST OF HEARTS.

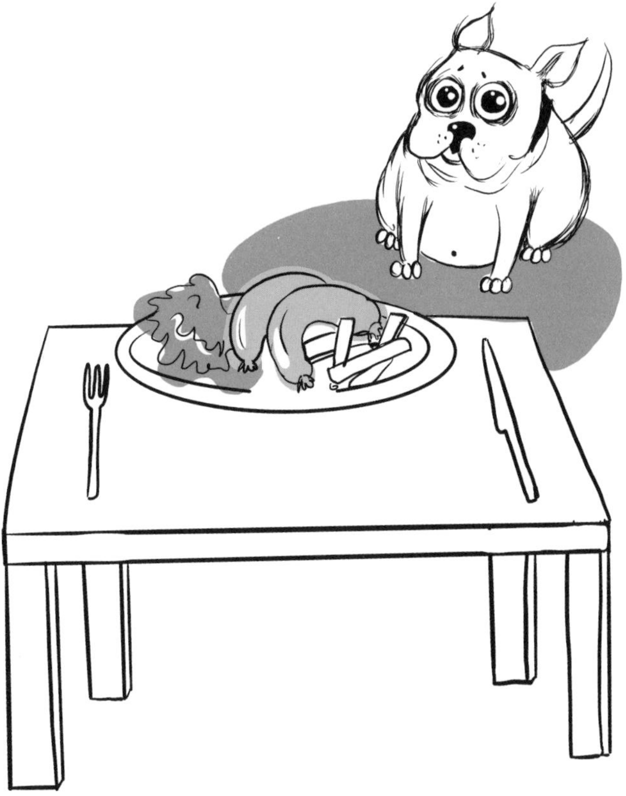

**THINK CAREFULLY
BEFORE ALLOWING**

THEM ON YOUR BED.

THE FIRST RULE OF BIN CLUB IS: YOUR DOG MUST SNIFF AND/OR PEE ON EVERY BIN.

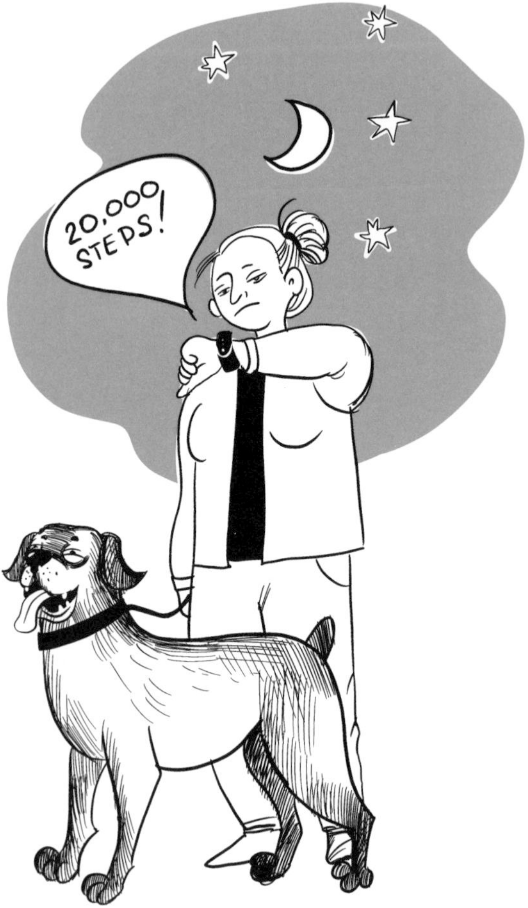
20,000 STEPS!

SETTING STEP-COUNT
GOALS IS A GREAT
WAY OF CONVINCING
YOURSELF THAT ALL
THESE DOG WALKS
ARE *YOUR* CHOICE.

**TELL YOUR
FRIENDS IT'S
A NEW DANCE
YOU TAUGHT HIM:**

THE BUTT SHUFFLE!

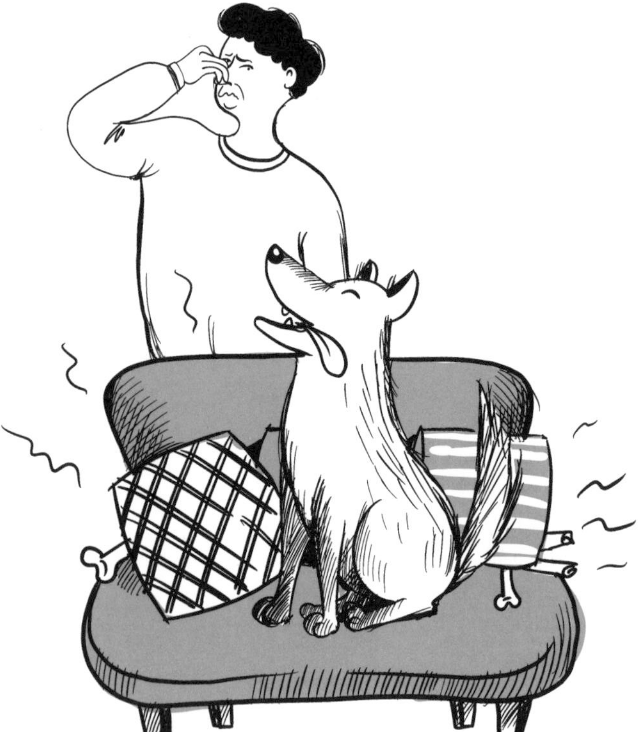

YOUR SOFA IS
A SECRET TREASURE
TROVE OF DOG CHEWS,
BONES AND A PRECIOUS
BIT OF CHICKEN HIDDEN
FROM DINNER.

YOU'VE NEVER BEEN
ON SUCH GOOD TERMS
WITH YOUR POSTIE.

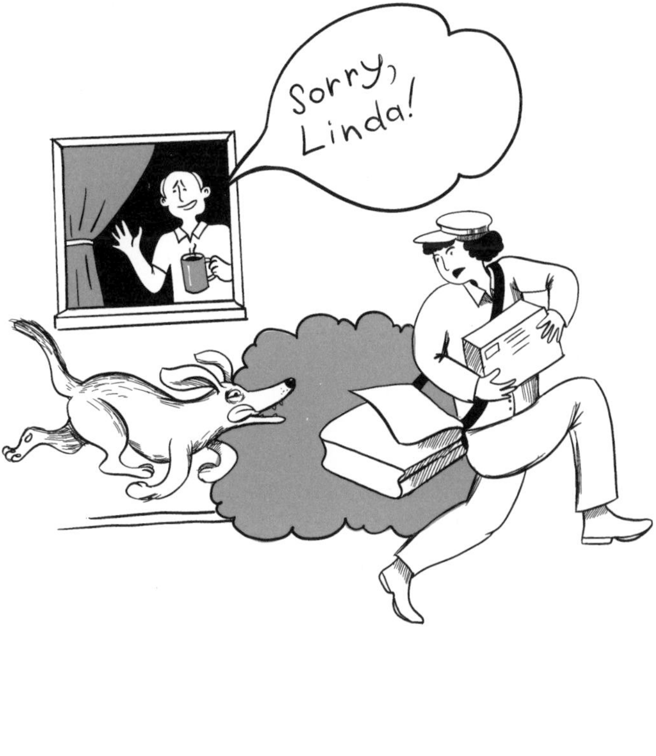
Sorry, Linda!

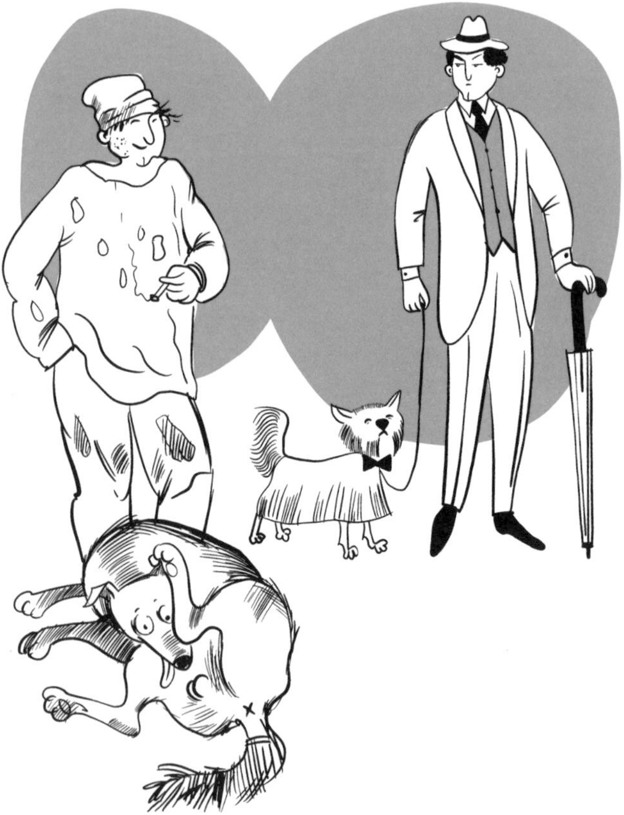

OTHER PEOPLE'S DOGS MAY LOOK

CLEANER AND

MORE WELL-BEHAVED THAN YOURS, BUT THEY PROBABLY

STILL HUMP THEIR OWNER'S LEGS

LIKE THE BEST OF THEM.

YOU MIGHT START
TO LOVE THEIR
STINKY BREATH.
TELL NO ONE.

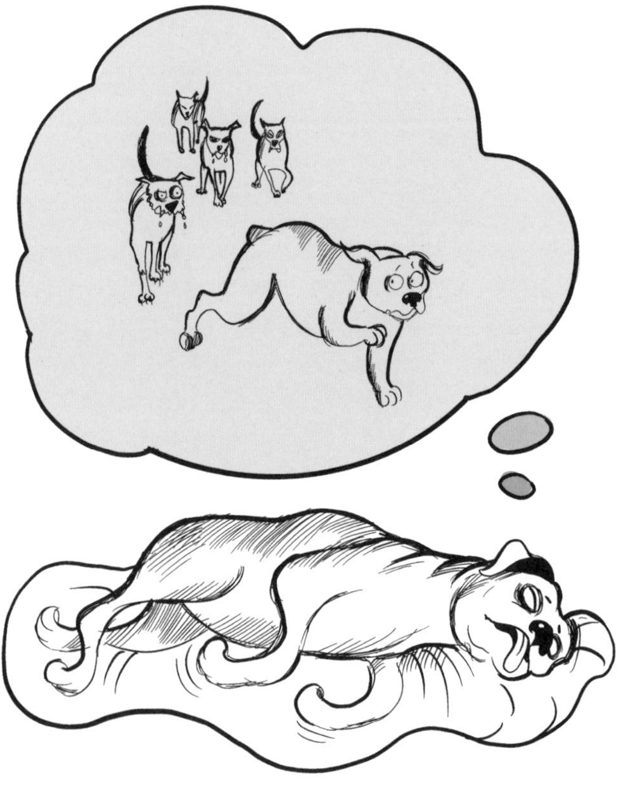

SURE, THEY MIGHT BE
DREAMING OF CHASING
SQUIRRELS... OR THEY
MIGHT BE DREAMING
ABOUT ZOMBIE PUPS!

THERE'LL ALWAYS BE A THIRD WHEEL

IN YOUR RELATIONSHIP.

YOU WILL NEVER TIRE OF
SHOWING OFF PICTURES
OF YOUR DOG BABY.

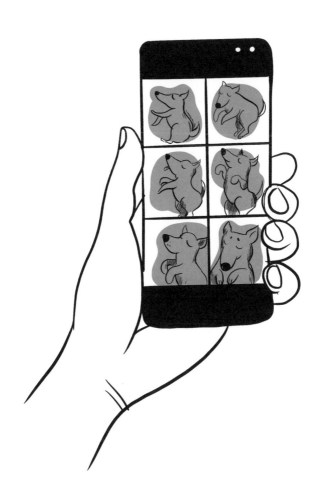

DOG HEAVEN IS...
POND WATER.

DOG HELL IS...

BATH WATER.

CONSIDER MOVING THE SOFA AWAY FROM THE WINDOW.

YOU CAN NEVER
SAY THE WORD
"SAUSAGE" OUT LOUD.

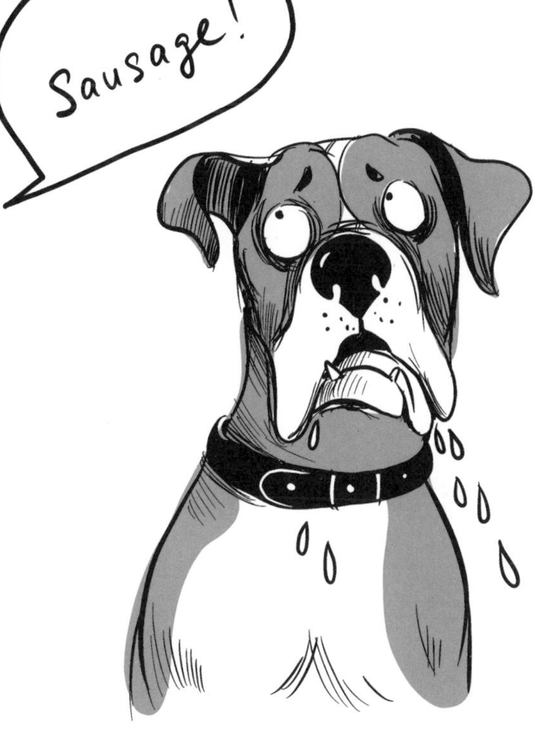
Sausage!

HOLD THE LEAD EXTRA-TIGHT WHEN SQUIRRELS

ARE ABOUT.

BEWARE THE
POWER OF A WAGGY TAIL.

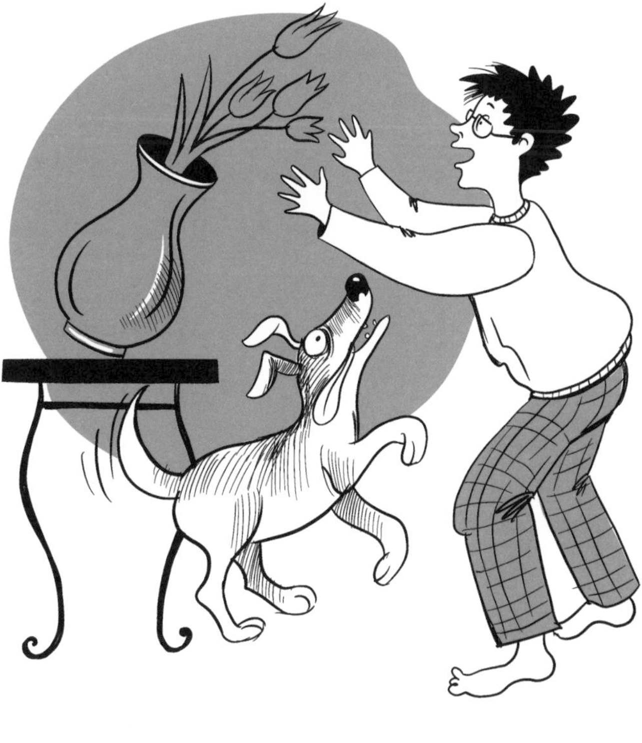

SOMETIMES YOU CAN'T
EVEN TEACH A *YOUNG*
DOG NEW TRICKS.

THERE'S NO WAY THEY
HAVE JUST HAD THEIR
NOSE UP ANOTHER

DOG'S BUTT.

THEY WOULDN'T
DO THAT.

WOULD THEY?

ONE OF THE BIGGEST
MORAL QUANDARIES IN
A DOG PARENT'S LIFE:
TO PICK UP AN
ABANDONED
POOP OR NOT.

THE VILLAGE'S
BEST-KEPT LAWN
AWARD WILL
NEVER GRACE YOUR
MANTELPIECE AGAIN.

DOG + STAIRS =
PERIL

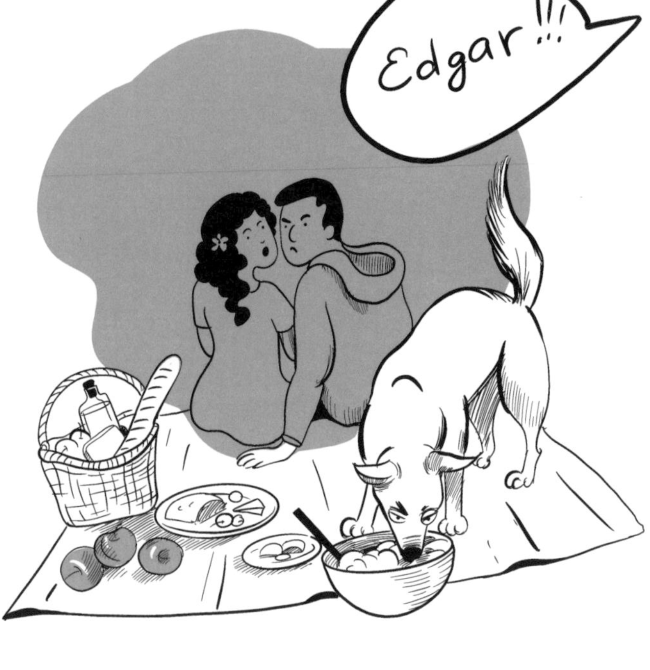
Edgar!!!

DOGS HAVE
SELECTIVE HEARING
– PARTICULARLY
WHEN THERE IS FOOD
IN THE VICINITY.

YOU CAN NEVER HAVE
ENOUGH STICKS.
I MEAN, YOU
COULD USE THEM
FOR A RUSTIC
UPCYCLING PROJECT.

YOU ONLY FED THE DOG

**TWO HANDFULS
OF KIBBLE,**

SO HOW COME
YOU NEED

THREE POOP BAGS

ON YOUR WALK?

PUDDLE WATER
TASTES THE BEST,
APPARENTLY.

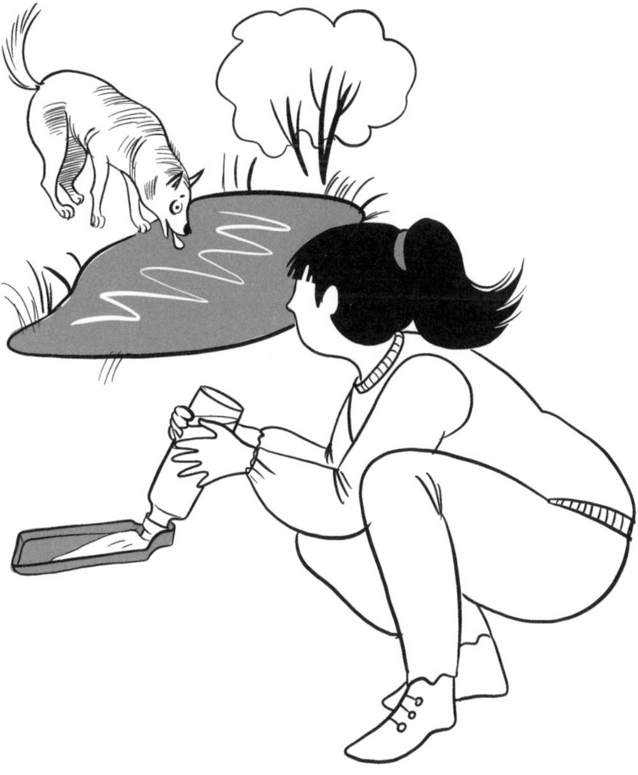

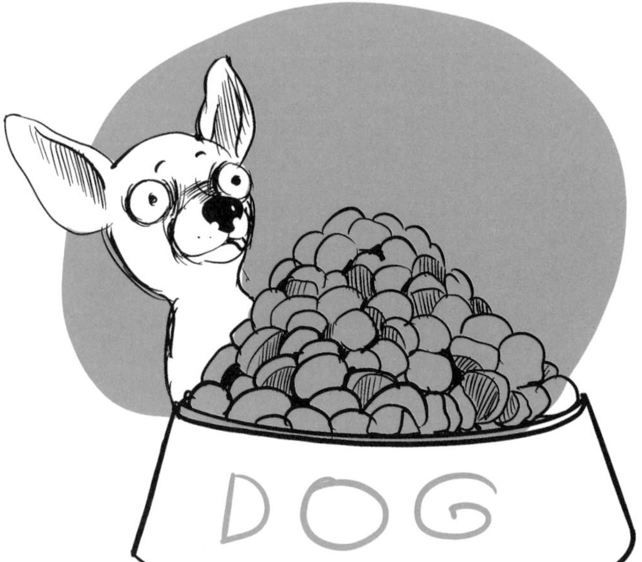
DOG

YOU'LL WONDER
HOW SO MUCH CHOW
CAN FIT INSIDE
SUCH A TINY DOG.

IF THERE'S A WIPEABLE VERSION,

BUY IT.

GET USED TO TALKING TO STRANGERS ABOUT DOGGY STYLE.

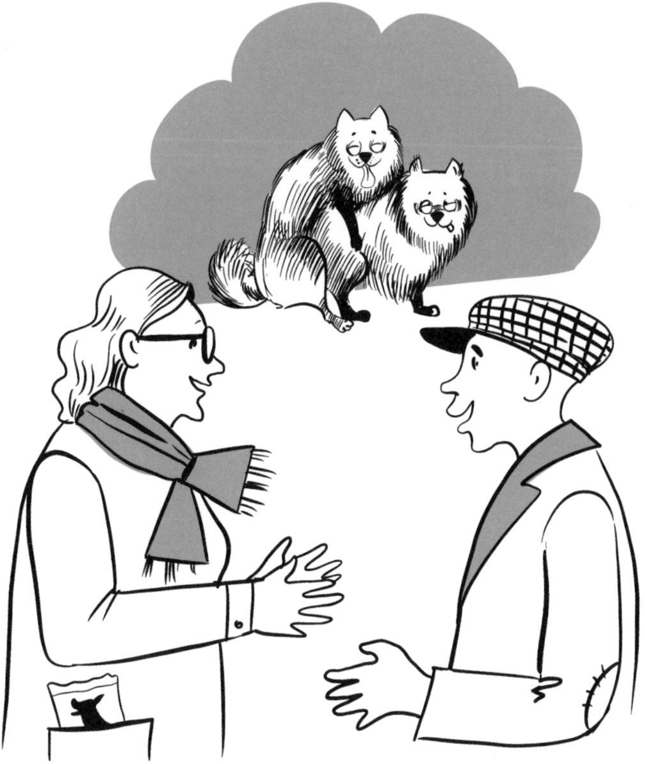

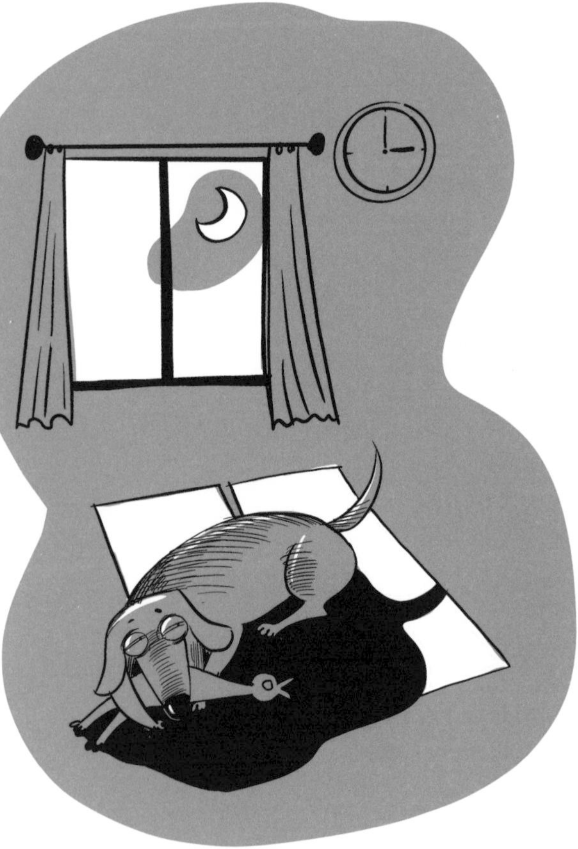

YOUR DOG WILL
IGNORE ITS NEW
SQUEAKY TOY.
UNTIL 3 A.M.

YOU HAVE BECOME THE

PROUD OWNER

OF THE
ALL-NEW ORGANIC

HAND-WARMER!

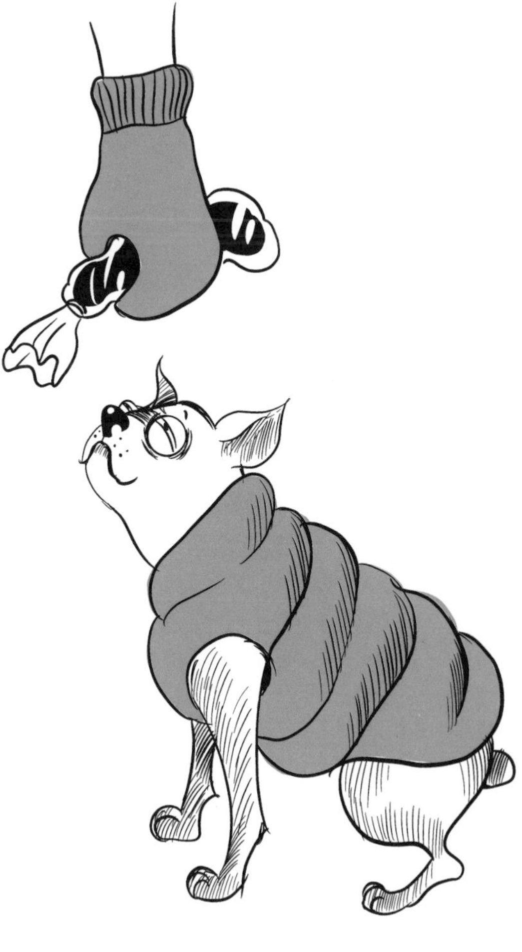

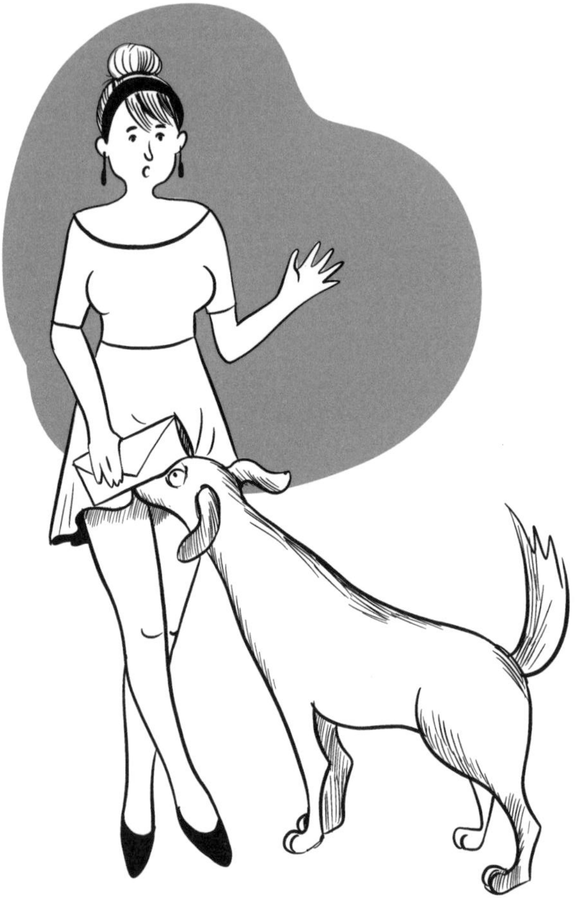

DON'T TAKE IT PERSONALLY.

IT IS A TRUTH UNIVERSALLY ACKNOWLEDGED THAT A DOG IN POSSESSION OF A HEALTHY LIBIDO MUST BE IN WANT OF A LEG.

A 10-MINUTE WALK NOW TAKES

HALF AN HOUR.

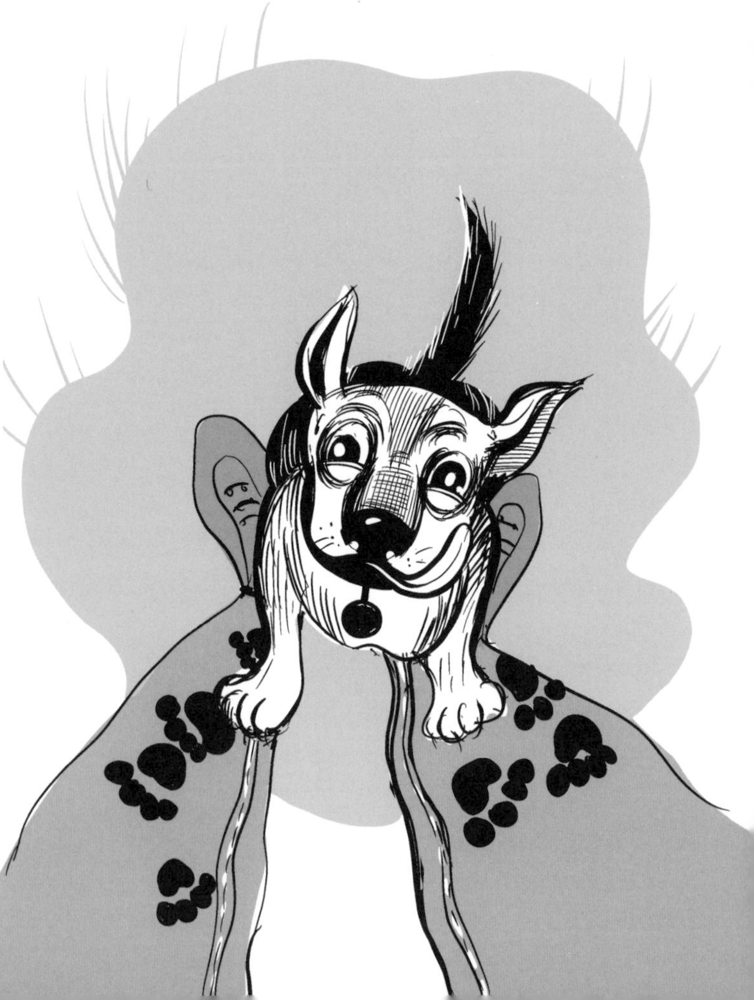

JUST CONVINCE
YOURSELF THAT
THIS SEASON'S
MUST-HAVE LOOK IS
PAW-PRINT THIGHS.

REMEMBER TO MAKE
SURE THE DOG IS IN THE
ROOM BEFORE BLAMING
YOUR FARTS ON THEM.

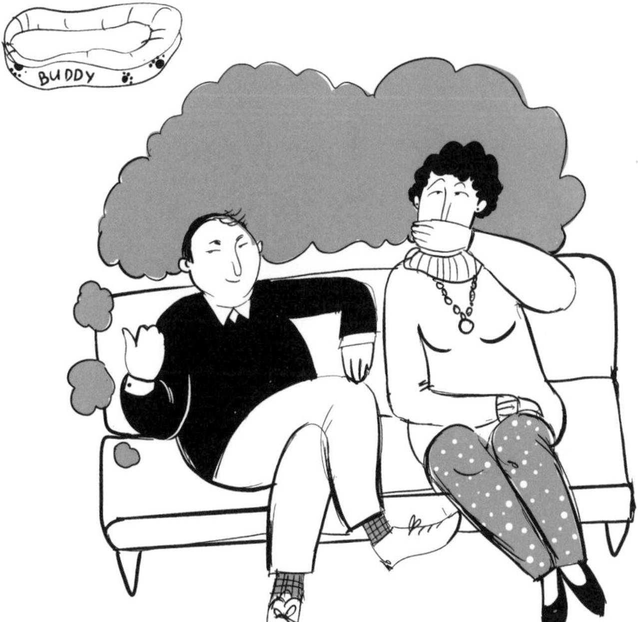
BUDDY

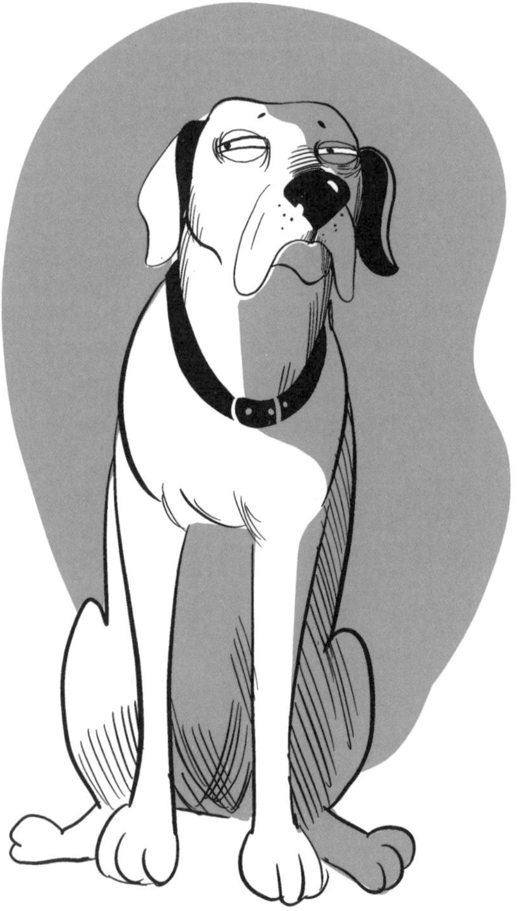

DON'T LET YOUR

DOG CATCH YOU

**GIVING AFFECTION
TO ANY OTHER
LIVING CREATURE,
UNLESS YOU ARE**

READY TO SUFFER

FROM "THE LOOK".

TAKE INSPIRATION FROM YOUR DOG. WHEN IN DOUBT, NAP.

MAYBE YOU COULD
DO SOMETHING WITH
YOUR DOG'S NATURAL
TALENT TO TANGLE?

**IT IS NO LONGER
SAFE TO LEAVE FOOD
UNSUPERVISED FOR**

EVEN A MOMENT.

ALLOW TIME FOR YOUR
DOG TO READ AND REPLY
TO THEIR PEE-MAILS.

YOU'VE REALIZED
THAT YOU'LL HAPPILY
PUT UP WITH ALL
OF THIS – BECAUSE
YOU LOVE THEM.

Have you enjoyed this book?

If so, find us on Facebook at
Summersdale Publishers, on Twitter
at @Summersdale and on Instagram
at @summersdalebooks and get in
touch. We'd love to hear from you!

www.summersdale.com